Romans, Reformers, Revolutionaries

A BIBLICAL WORLD HISTORY CURRICULUM
RESURRECTION TO REVOLUTION
AD 30–AD 1799

1:1
answersingenesis
Petersburg, Kentucky, USA

US $8.99

ISBN-10 1-60092-177-9
ISBN-13 978-1-60092-177-3

9 781600 921773

$8.09

73823

Answers in Genesis HISTORY written by Diana Waring

About this test kit

The Unit tests in this test kit cover the material taught in Phase 1. Since we approach history with the understanding that it is a vast, nearly limitless subject, it would be unreasonable to demand that every student know every aspect of what every other student learns. Therefore, a standard history test of names, dates, and places is not adequate for this curriculum, nor will it display the particulars and the depth of what each student has learned. For this reason, we have created questions in these Unit tests, which allow the student to choose areas with which he or she is familiar. We also highly recommend using a rubric grid (such as the one shown in the Teacher Guide introduction) to provide a fair assessment of the creative work of each student, which is an additional and significant means of evaluating what a student has learned in Phases 2, 3, and 4.

Making copies from this test kit

You may make copies of this kit if

- you (or someone in your organization) are the original purchaser;

- you are using the copies for a noncommercial purpose (such as teaching or promoting your organization) within your organization;

Permission to make photocopies of or to reproduce by any other mechanical or electronic means in whole or in part any designated page, illustration, or activity in this book is granted only to the original purchaser and is intended for noncommercial use within a home, church, school, or other Christian organization. None of the material in this book may be reproduced for any commercial promotion, advertising, or sale of a product or service or to share with any other persons, churches, or organizations. Sharing of the material in this book with other organizations not owned or controlled by the original purchaser is also prohibited. All rights reserved.

Romans, Reformers, Revolutionaries: Resurrection to Revolution: Test Kit

Copyright 2008 Diana Waring. Permission to photocopy granted.

For more information, contact
Answers in Genesis
2800 Bullittsburg Church Rd.
Petersburg, KY 41080

All Scripture quotations are taken from the New King James Version, © 1979, 1980, 1982 by Thomas Nelson, Inc., Publishers. Used by permission.

Cover Design: Brandie Lucas
Text Design: Diane King
Editor: Gary Vaterlaus

Printed in the United States of America.

www.answersingenesis.org

Unit 1 Test
The Rise of the Church & the Fall of Rome

Name: _____   Date: _____

1. Choose **two** of the five Key Concepts below from this Unit with which you are most familiar. For each of these two concepts, list at least two of the most important facts related to that concept.

    - The gospel to the Jews & Gentiles
    - The Roman emperors
    - The growth of the persecuted church

    - Dividing & defending the empire
    - Reasons for the fall of Rome

2. If you believe the statement below to be true, explain why and back up your reasons with as much historical and biblical data as possible. If you believe the statement to be false, explain why and back up your reasons with as much historical and biblical data as possible.

    "Constantine allowed and promoted Christianity in the Empire because of his own faith in the Christian God."

3. Match each key person, place, or event on the left side of the page with the short description on the right side of the page.

_____ Nero   a. AD 70

_____ Council of Nicaea   b. Document giving legal status to Christianity

_____ Jerome   c. Martyred under Nero

_____ Constantine   d. Translated the Latin Vulgate

_____ Destruction of Jerusalem   e. Blamed Christians for burning of Rome

_____ Constantinople   f. Extended the Empire to its furthest reach

_____ Apostle Paul   g. Capital of the Eastern Empire

_____ Diocletian   h. AD 325

_____ Trajan   i. First Christian Emperor

_____ Edict of Milan   j. Launched last and greatest persecution of the Church

4. Choose **two** of the following and answer them with a short 1 to 2 paragraph answer.

- What would you say to someone who does not believe the Resurrection actually occurred?
- Explain what made the indwelling of the Holy Spirit on the Day of Pentecost a new era in history.
- Why did Domitian launch the second great persecution of the Church in the AD 90s?
- What were the characteristics of Greco-Roman cities of the time?
- What made Emperor Diocletian significant?

Unit 2 Test
Missionaries & Barbarians

Name: _____   Date: _____

1. Choose **two** of the five Key Concepts below from this Unit with which you are most familiar. For each of these two concepts, list at least two of the most important facts related to that concept.

   - Motivations for invasion
   - Barbarians' impact on the West
   - The Church's response

   - Celtic missionaries
   - Celtic Christianity

2. If you believe the statement below to be true, explain why and back up your reasons with as much historical and biblical data as possible. If you believe the statement to be false, explain why and back up your reasons with as much historical and biblical data as possible.

   "As pagan barbarians invaded the West, Christians preserved both literature and literacy."

3. Match each key person, place, or event on the left side of the page with the short description on the right side of the page.

_____ Patrick   a. Missionary to Scotland

_____ Attila the Hun   b. Evangelized northern England

_____ King Arthur   c. Founded monastic order

_____ Foederati   d. Sacked Rome in 455

_____ Columba   e. Missionary to Ireland

_____ Benedict   f. "Scourge of God"

_____ Visigoths   g. England chose to follow Roman Christianity

_____ Synod of Whitby   h. Mercenaries subsidized by Rome

_____ Vandals   i. Sacked Rome in 410

_____ Aidan   j. Legendary king who defended Britain

4. Choose **two** of the following and answer them with a short 1 to 2 paragraph answer.

   • Who was King Arthur and who did he fight?

   • Who was Clovis, what led to his conversion, and what were the effects of it?

   • Why was this period called the "Dark Ages," and how might this be a misnomer?

   • What made the Visigoth's sack of Rome in 410 different, and what was the response from secular rulers and Christians?

Unit 3 Test
The Byzantines & Muslims

Name: _____   Date: _____

1. Choose **two** of the five Key Concepts below from this Unit with which you are most familiar. For each of these two concepts, list at least two of the most important facts related to that concept.

  - Orthodox vs. Roman Christianity
  - Rise of Islam
  - Byzantine civilization

  - Seven ecumenical councils
  - Islamic civilization

2. If you believe the statement below to be true, explain why and back up your reasons with as much historical and biblical data as possible. If you believe the statement to be false, explain why and back up your reasons with as much historical and biblical data as possible.

  "The state-run nature of the Orthodox Church (rather than individual commitments to Jesus) can explain the brutal doctrinal schisms that riddle this era."

3. Match each key person, place, or event on the left side of the page with the short description on the right side of the page.

_____ Nestorianism	a. Debate over the use of icons
_____ Mohammed	b. Eastern Roman Empire
_____ Iconoclast Controversy	c. Christ has only one nature
_____ Justinian I	d. Capital city of the early Islamic Empire
_____ Baghdad	e. Golden-mouthed preacher
_____ Photius the Great	f. Franks defeated Muslim army
_____ Monophysitism	g. Christ exists as two persons
_____ Battle of Tours	h. Founder of Islam
_____ John Chrysostom	i. "Wisest man of the Middle Ages"
_____ Byzantine Empire	j. Greatest Byzantine emperor

4. Choose **two** of the following and answer them with a short 1 to 2 paragraph answer.

- Why did the Byzantine emperors have so much power, and what effect did it have on their reigns?

- What makes Justinian I one of the greatest of the Byzantine emperors?

- What was the religious environment that Mohammed was born into and how might it have affected him?

- Trace the course of power in the Islamic Empire after Mohammed's death.

- Compare the cities of Constantinople and Baghdad—in what ways are they similar, in what different?

Unit 4 Test
The Holy Roman Empire
& the Vikings

Name: _____   Date: _____

1. Choose **two** of the four Key Concepts below from this Unit with which you are most familiar. For each of these two concepts, list at least two of the most important facts related to that concept.

- Holy Roman Empire
- Viking invasions & explorations
- Norman conquest
- Struggle between Church & State

2. If you believe the statement below to be true, explain why and back up your reasons with as much historical and biblical data as possible. If you believe the statement to be false, explain why and back up your reasons with as much historical and biblical data as possible.

"William the Conqueror was justified in his assault on England."

3. Match each key person, place, or event on the left side of the page with the short description on the right side of the page.

_____ Charlemagne   a. Missionaries to the Slavs

_____ Leif Ericson   b. Church laws regulating warfare

_____ Cyril & Methodius   c. Norman king of England

_____ Treaty of Verdun   d. Carried out by Abbot Odo

_____ Vikings   e. Norse warriors who raided Europe

_____ Great Schism   f. King of the Franks

_____ Cluniac Reform   g. 1054

_____ William the Conqueror   h. Norse explorer

_____ Peace & Truce of God   i. Divided the Empire into three kingdoms

_____ Alfred the Great   j. Founder of English nation

4. Choose **two** of the following and answer them with a short 1 to 2 paragraph answer.

- What was so significant about Pope Leo III's action on Christmas Day, 800?
- What led up to the Treaty of Verdun, and what was its effect?
- What made King Alfred of England different from his western contemporaries?
- What were the methods and motives of the Viking raiders?
- How did feudalism work?

Unit 5 Test
The Crusades & the Mongols

Name: _____   Date: _____

1. Choose **two** of the five Key Concepts below from this Unit with which you are most familiar. For each of these two concepts, list at least two of the most important facts related to that concept.

- The Crusades
- Catholic reformers
- Medieval dissenters

- The West in Constantinople
- The Mongols

2. If you believe the statement below to be true, explain why and back up your reasons with as much historical and biblical data as possible. If you believe the statement to be false, explain why and back up your reasons with as much historical and biblical data as possible.

"The Medieval crusades could be conceived of as a type of Christian *jihad*."

3. Match each key person, place, or event on the left side of the page with the short description on the right side of the page.

_____ Pope Urban II   a. "Holy" wars to rescue the Holy Land from Muslims

_____ Investiture Controversy   b. Special tribunal to combat and punish heresy

_____ Thomas Aquinas   c. Venetian explorer who went to China

_____ Magna Carta   d. Mongolian conqueror

_____ Marco Polo   e. Muslim leader who took Jerusalem

_____ Francis of Assisi   f. Charter of English political and civil liberties

_____ The Crusades   g. Started the First Crusade

_____ Genghis Khan   h. Power struggle between papacy and Holy Roman Empire

_____ Inquisition   i. Catholic philosopher/theologian

_____ Saladin   j. Founder of monastic order

4. Choose **two** of the following and answer them with a short 1 to 2 paragraph answer.

- Describe the change in papal-royal relations.
- Describe the divisions within the Islamic Empire.
- Compare/contrast the first Crusade to the later ones.
- In what ways did King John (brother of Richard the Lionheart) leave his mark on England?
- How did Marco Polo's adventures in China affect Europe?

Unit 6 Test
Seeds of the Reformation &
the Late Middle Ages

Name: _____   Date: _____

1. Choose **two** of the five Key Concepts below from this Unit with which you are most familiar. For each of these two concepts, list at least two of the most important facts related to that concept.

- Hundred Years' War
- Western Church in Crisis
- The printing press

- Exploration & trade
- Fall of Constantinople

2. If you believe the statement below to be true, explain why and back up your reasons with as much historical and biblical data as possible. If you believe the statement to be false, explain why and back up your reasons with as much historical and biblical data as possible.

"The relocation of the popes to Avignon opened the door to the Reformation."

3. Match each key person, place, or event on the left side of the page with the short description on the right side of the page.

_____ John Wycliffe   a. Wars fought between England and France

_____ Henry the Navigator   b. Ruler of the Ottomans

_____ Johannes Gutenberg   c. Sent ships down African coast

_____ Avignon   d. Captured Constantinople

_____ Ottomans   e. Lifted the siege of Orleans

_____ Mehmet II   f. 25 million people died in Europe

_____ Joan of Arc   g. Bohemian reformer and martyr

_____ Hundred Years' War   h. Translated the Bible into English

_____ John Hus   i. Seat of seven Popes in the 1300s

_____ Black Plague   j. Invented the printing press

4. Choose **two** of the following and answer them with a short 1 to 2 paragraph answer.

- What specific examples show how the power of kings decreased from absolute to something less in this age?

- Map out the main players in the conflict between Scotland and England, which provides motivations for the Hundred Years' War between England and France.

- Summarize John Wycliffe's life and work. What made him stand out in the contemporary Church?

- How did Joan of Arc aid France during the Hundred Years' War?

- What was the impact of the Black Plague in Europe?

Unit 7 Test
The Renaissance &
the Reformation

Name: _____   Date: _____

1. Choose **two** of the five Key Concepts below from this Unit with which you are most familiar. For each of these two concepts, list at least two of the most important facts related to that concept.

   - The Renaissance
   - The Reformation
   - The Age of Exploration
   - The New World
   - The Scientific Revolution

2. If you believe the statement below to be true, explain why and back up your reasons with as much historical and biblical data as possible. If you believe the statement to be false, explain why and back up your reasons with as much historical and biblical data as possible.

   "The Reformation has had a greater continuing impact on history than the Renaissance."

3. Match each key person, place, or event on the left side of the page with the short description on the right side of the page.

_____ Erasmus   a. Taught heliocentric theory

_____ Martin Luther   b. Convened to condemn teachings of reformers

_____ Nicolaus Copernicus   c. Translated English Bible

_____ Council of Trent   d. Opened route to New World

_____ Jesuits   e. French reformer

_____ The Reformation   f. First to circumnavigate the earth

_____ William Tyndale   g. Initially to reform Catholic Church

_____ Christopher Columbus   h. Catalyst of the Protestant Reformation

_____ Ferdinand Magellan   i. Monastic order founded by Ignatius Loyola

_____ John Calvin   j. Compiled Greek New Testament

4. Choose **two** of the following and answer them with a short 1 to 2 paragraph answer.

- Describe Charles V, and the circumstances at the beginning of his rule.

- Who is Martin Luther, and what were the radical changes he brought to light?

- What is the significance of Henry VIII?

- Compare/contrast Portugal's experience in exploration and trade to Spain's experience.

Unit 8 Test
Puritans, Pietists, & the Divine Right of Kings

Name: _____ Date: _____

1. Choose **two** of the five Key Concepts below from this Unit with which you are most familiar. For each of these two concepts, list at least two of the most important facts related to that concept.

- Europe's Thirty Years' War
- British colonization of the New World
- Galileo & Newton

- The Puritan revolution
- Pietism

2. If you believe the statement below to be true, explain why and back up your reasons with as much historical and biblical data as possible. If you believe the statement to be false, explain why and back up your reasons with as much historical and biblical data as possible.

"France brought assistance to the Protestants in the Thirty Years' War for religious reasons."

3. Match each key person, place, or event on the left side of the page with the short description on the right side of the page.

_____ John Bunyan   a. The Sun King

_____ Pilgrims   b. Reformer of Russia

_____ Edict of Nantes   c. Pioneered telescope in astronomy

_____ Blaise Pascal   d. Lord Protector of England

_____ Louis XIV   e. Came to North America seeking religious freedom

_____ Thirty Years' War   f. Granted rights to Protestants of France

_____ Galileo Galilei   g. A monarch derives his right to rule from God

_____ Peter the Great   h. Author of *The Pilgrim's Progress*

_____ Divine Right of Kings i. French Christian mathematician

_____ Oliver Cromwell   j. Religious war in Germany

4. Choose **two** of the following and answer them with a short 1 to 2 paragraph answer.

- Why did the Catholic church condemn Galileo and sentence him to imprisonment, and what can we learn from this episode?
- Why did the English Parliament execute Charles I in 1649?
- How did Elizabeth I's Act of Uniformity contribute to the rise of the Puritan movement?
- How were the Separatists different from the Puritans?
- What is the basic idea behind the Divine Right of Kings?

Unit 9 Test
Revivals & Revolutions

Name: _____   Date: _____

1. Choose **two** of the five Key Concepts below from this Unit with which you are most familiar. For each of these two concepts, list at least two of the most important facts related to that concept.

- The Enlightenment
- The Great Awakening & beginning of abolition
- The Seven Years' War

- Revolutions in France & America
- Cook's voyages

2. If you believe the statement below to be true, explain why and back up your reasons with as much historical and biblical data as possible. If you believe the statement to be false, explain why and back up your reasons with as much historical and biblical data as possible.

"The Great Awakening paved the way for many of the ideas of the American Revolution."

3. Match each key person, place, or event on the left side of the page with the short description on the right side of the page.

_____ Jonathan Edwards   a. Evangelist of Great Awakening

_____ The Seven Years' War b. Invented the steam engine

_____ George Whitefield   c. Famous explorer

_____ Charles Wesley   d. Empress of Russia

_____ John Newton   e. American colonial theologian

_____ Great Awakening   f. Slave ship captain turned preacher

_____ Captain Cook   g. Religious revival in England and America

_____ Catherine the Great   h. Cofounder of Methodism and hymn writer

_____ George Washington   i. Resulted in England winning French colonial lands

_____ James Watt   j. First U.S. President

4. Choose **two** of the following and answer them with a short 1 to 2 paragraph answer.

- What were the main elements of "Enlightenment" thinking?
- What were the main differences between the American Revolution and the French Revolution?
- Relate some of the accomplishments of John Wesley.
- Why did Prussia go to war against Austria?

Unit 1 Test
The Rise of the Church & the Fall of Rome

1. Choose **two** of the five Key Concepts below from this Unit with which you are most familiar. For each of these two concepts, list at least two of the most important facts related to that concept. [*Some possible answers are listed below. Accept any reasonable points that were discussed in the reading or audio lessons.*]

The gospel to the Jews and Gentiles

- Jesus's Resurrection
- The Great Commission
- Outpouring of the Holy Spirit at Pentecost
- Political unity of the Empire allowed freedom of travel for Christians
- Paul's missionary journeys
- The gospel went to Europe, Africa, and Asia in the first century AD.

The Roman emperors

- Persecuted the Church, but God used it to display the courage and obedience of His followers
- Eventually caused Christianity to be legalized
- Led sordid and unhappy lives; contrast with the King of Kings and the Christians
- The personalities of the leaders effected major change on the state of the Empire

The growth of the persecuted Church

- Possible partly because of the era in history when infrastructure and communication were greatly increased from the previous centuries
- Witness to God's faithfulness in the midst of struggle
- Character of Christian martyrs had in impact on others
- Christians' kind actions during the Antonine Plague made an impression on people
- Christians began defending the tenets of Christianity through *apologetics* to those in the Roman Empire

Dividing & defending the Empire

- Many emperors struggled to maintain the success of their predecessors
- Diocletian divided the Empire because he saw it was necessary to maintain order
- Diocletian appointed two Augusti, two Caesars, and 12 vicars over each of the 12 dioceses
- Emperors made the decision to employ barbarian soldiers in the Roman Army, which eventually had negative effects

Reasons for the fall of Rome

- Division of the Empire
- Empire spread beyond its capacity to maintain
- Theodosius made Visigoths allies of Rome, allowing them to settle inside Roman territory;

they later overthrew Rome
  - The fall of Rome was not the fall of the Church

2. "Constantine allowed and promoted Christianity in the Empire because of his own faith in the Christian God." [*Students may choose to view this question as true or false, depending on their point of view. However, if they are able to adequately support their view, even if it differs from that of the author, then the answer should be evaluated on the display of the student's understanding of the issues.*]

  - This statement may be argued as true of false. Arguments for the genuineness of Constantine's faith include the fact that he was generous towards others with his money, he had a deep sense of justice as a ruler, and he was morally pure in the area of sexuality. He forbade crucifixion and banned the branding of criminals on the face. He passed a law making Sunday—the Christian day of worshipping God—an official day of rest. He called the Council of Nicaea to deal with an ongoing struggle in the Church concerning whether Jesus was the same as God.

  - On the other hand, Constantine was vain about his appearance and subject to flattery, and chose to follow Diocletian's style of being emperor—with great pomp and circumstance, wearing a jeweled diadem to show how exalted the emperor was, living quite above and quite distantly from his subjects. In his later years, Constantine became increasingly suspicious about the loyalty of people close to him—putting many people to death, including his own wife and one of his sons. Those are certainly not the actions of a true believer. It's hard to know from this distance, but one way or another, Constantine brought a startling and dramatic change to the Roman Empire and to Christianity.

3. Match each key person, place, or event on the left side of the page with the short description on the right side of the page.

_e_ Nero		a. AD 70
_h_ Council of Nicaea		b. Document giving legal status to Christianity
_d_ Jerome		c. Martyred under Nero
_i_ Constantine		d. Translated the Latin Vulgate
_a_ Destruction of Jerusalem		e. Blamed Christians for burning of Rome
_g_ Constantinople		f. Extended the Empire to its furthest reach
_c_ Apostle Paul		g. Capital of the Eastern Empire
_j_ Diocletian		h. AD 325
_f_ Trajan		i. First Christian Emperor
_b_ Edict of Milan		j. Launched last and greatest persecution of the Church

4. Choose **two** of the following questions and answer them with a short 1 to 2 paragraph answer. [*The essays written by the student will probably contain at least a few of the following points. If you are unfamiliar with the points actually made by the student, please ask for the sources.*]

What would you say to someone who does not believe the Resurrection actually occurred?
  - The New Testament is a reliable historical document
  - There is no other adequate explanation for the empty tomb

- There were over 500 witnesses to Jesus's Resurrection
- The changed lives of the disciples points to the truth of the Resurrection

Explain what made the indwelling of the Holy Spirit on the Day of Pentecost a new era in history.
- God now dwelt bodily in humans
- Transformed apostles to be fearless evangelists
- Power of God demonstrated in observers' own language
- Signs to contemporary unbelievers
- Launched spread of gospel outside of the Jewish community

Why did Domitian launch the second great persecution of the Church in the AD 90s?
- He had taken title "Lord and God"
- Imperial cult of worshipping the emperor
- Common to worship many gods, which was threatened by Christians' belief in only one God
- Emperor worship means of instilling and verifying loyalty in diverse Empire
- Decreed Christianity as *atheism*

What were the characteristics of Greco-Roman cities of the time?
- Very small in area and dense in population
- Families lived in one-room dwellings in tenement housing
- Cooking done over brazier inside; no chimneys
- Frequent city fires
- Public baths and toilets
- Limited access to water and sanitation
- Crime, fear, ethnic hatred, recurring wars, the Plague

What made Emperor Diocletian significant?
- Saw weakness of one-ruler system over Empire
- Divided imperial authority between two Augusti and two Caesars
- Reorganized Empire into 12 "dioceses," each with a "vicar" to govern it
- Rome no longer the imperial city
- Instituted the great empire-wide persecution of Christians in 303
- Daughter and wife favorable to Christianity
- Persecution did not end until AD 311

Unit 2 Test
Missionaries & Barbarians

1. Choose **two** of the five Key Concepts below from this Unit with which you are most familiar. For each of these two concepts, list at least two of the most important facts related to that concept. [*Some possible answers are listed below. Accept any reasonable points that were discussed in the reading or audio lessons.*]

Motivations for Invasion
- Desire to partake of the wealth evidenced in the Roman Empire
- Proximity and fear of the Huns brought nearby tribes into Empire
- Mistreatment of barbarians by the Romans caused them to revolt
- Power vacuum in Roman leadership invited Visigoth rule

Barbarians' Impact on the West
- "Mass conversion" style of Christianity resulted in pagan practices, beliefs in the church
- Reordered geopolitical lines and languages
- Changed from highly structured, highly developed Empire to various lands settled by illiterate Germanic tribes
- Ushered in the so-called "Dark Ages"

The Church's Response
- Pope Leo I persuaded Attila to turn from the city of Rome
- Main concern of Early Medieval Church (425–1054) to survive invasions
- Spread the gospel to Arian and pagan tribes
- Monasticism became prominent in the Church

Celtic Missionaries
- Took gospel to fierce tribes (starting with Patrick to his captors, the Celts)
- Columba took missionaries to Iona in Scotland
- Columbanus brought gospel to barbarians in Europe: Gaul, Switzerland, Italy
- Possessed a unique passion for foreign missions
- The peregrini (wandering monks of the Celtic church, both men and women)
- Reestablished literacy in many places in Europe and took books wherever they went

Celtic Christianity
- Celtic monks traveled as missionaries
- Celtic abbots in charge of each monastery; no ruler over all
- Date of Easter differed from Romans
- Style of tonsure differed from Romans
- Nature of bishop's travel differed from Romans

2. "As pagan barbarians invaded the West, Christians preserved both literature and literacy." [*Students may choose to view this question as true or false, depending on their point of view. However, if they are able to adequately support their view, even if it differs from that of the author, then the answer should be evaluated on the display of the student's understanding of the issues*.]

- True. In both Celtic and Roman monasteries, there was a high value placed on the Scriptures and other books. Because of this, select monks were trained in reading and writing so that they would be able to make copies for preservation and distribution. As monks established monasteries throughout Europe, they were also setting up key centers for perpetuating literacy and education.

3. Match each key person, place, or event on the left side of the page with the short description on the right side of the page.

__e__ Patrick	a. Missionary to Scotland
__f__ Attila the Hun	b. Evangelized northern England
__j__ King Arthur	c. Founded monastic order
__h__ Foederati	d. Sacked Rome in 455
__a__ Columba	e. Missionary to Ireland
__c__ Benedict	f. "Scourge of God"
__i__ Visigoths	g. England chose to follow Roman Christianity
__g__ Synod of Whitby	h. Mercenaries subsidized by Rome
__d__ Vandals	i. Sacked Rome in 410
__b__ Aidan	j. Legendary king who defended Britain

4. Choose **two** of the following questions and answer them with a short 1 to 2 paragraph answer. [*The essays written by the student will probably contain at least a few of the following points. If you are unfamiliar with the points actually made by the student, please ask for the sources.*]

Who was King Arthur and who did he fight?
- The Angles & Saxons invited up to stave off the fierce Picts & Celts; once they arrived, they never left
- King Arthur was a native Briton, a Christian, and a warrior in the Roman style
- He was commander of mobile field cavalry army against Saxon infantry
- He is considered the last Roman

Who was Clovis, what led to his conversion, and what were the effects of it?
- Ruler of the powerful Germanic tribe of Franks
- Married Catholic (non-Arian) Christian princess Clothilda
- On eve of losing battle, swore to follow God if granted victory
- Upon winning, was baptized with 3,000 of his warriors
- Because Catholic, many of the people under his rule accepted him in a way they never accepted Germanic barbarians (Arian Christians)
- Romans in Gaul gave their Catholic leader full support so he could defeat Arian Visigoths
- Eventually conquered all of modern day France
- Provided greater foothold for Roman Catholic influences throughout the area

Why was this period called the "Dark Ages," and how might this be a misnomer?

- So-called because center of power shifted from light and airy Mediterranean to gloomy wilds of northern Europe
- Also because the highly structured and highly developed Empire reordered under diverse and smaller Germanic tribal rulers
- Many areas lost their written history and literacy with the arrival of non-written tribal culture
- However, this was a time of great light through the monasteries, both Roman and Celtic
- Celtic monks brought books and literacy everywhere they preached
- Benedict monks fled Italy to bring the Benedictine Rules to monasteries throughout Europe
- The embrace of Christianity by tribes brought peace and a major decrease in atrocities

What made the Visigoth's sack of Rome in 410 different, and what was the response from secular rulers and Christians?

- Visigoths were Arian Christians from Ulfila's missionary work
- City itself not physically devastated
- Much less massacres than those of conquerors like Attila and Alexander
- Churches and people seeking refuge there spared
- Pagan intellectuals blamed Christians, and forsaken gods taking retribution
- Augustine of Hippo pointed out that barbarians spared people who sought refuge
- Bad things happened during Punic Wars and the old gods had not spared Rome
- Christians suffered along with pagans in the sacking

Unit 3 Test
The Byzantines & Muslims

1. Choose **two** of the five Key Concepts below from this Unit with which you are most familiar. For each of these two concepts, list at least two of the most important facts related to that concept. [*Some possible answers are listed below. Accept any reasonable points that were discussed in the reading or audio lessons.*]

Orthodox vs. Roman Christianity

- Orthodox used the Greek language (more focused on ideas); Roman Catholic spoke Latin (more focused on rhetoric)
- Orthodox Christians looked to one leader—the Byzantine Emperor—as their earthly ruler who had priestly functions; Roman Christians looked to the pope and emperor separately
- Orthodox set up five patriarchs to share guidance of the Church; Romans look only to the Pope

Rise of Islam

- Before Mohammed, Arabs were individual groups of tribal people
- Mohammed born in Mecca in 569 amidst many religious groups
- Mecca important religious and trading city
- Mohammed fled to Medina in 622 in the Hegira (flight from Mecca)
- After the Hegira, Mohammed said the sword is key to heaven and hell
- Belief in fatalism ("will of Allah") and Paradise for death in battle
- Belief system made Muslim warriors unstoppable
- Within one hundred years, Muslims had conquered much of Byzantine Empire, including North Africa and the Holy Land, and even Spain
- Under various Caliphs, attempts to conquer Constantinople
- Within 200 years, Islamic Empire's wealth exceeded that of the Byzantines

Seven Ecumenical Councils

- Orthodox church concerned about doctrinal subtleties
- Hotly debated at all levels of society
- Councils held to officially settle issues of doctrine/heresy
- Many splits occurred afterward:
  » Council of Ephesus: Nestorians split to Persia (where welcomed for being anti-Byzantine)
  » Council of Chalcedon: Monophysites split (became Coptic Church, among others)

Byzantine Civilization

- Greek speakers
- Despising and despised by Western Europeans
- Centered in modern-day Istanbul, in gold-adorned Constantinople
- Strategic location between the West and East Asia; much wealth
- Ruler had absolute power; believed to be continuing the rule of whole Roman Empire

Unit 3 Answers

Islamic Civilization
- Cultural and religious unity
- Cultural seat in Baghdad; built in four years by 100,000 laborers
- Known for colleges, hospitals, and hotels
- The arts and sciences flourished
- Baghdad became greatest trading port in history

2. "The state-run nature of the Orthodox Church (rather than individual commitments to Jesus) can explain the brutal doctrinal schisms that riddle this era." [*Students may choose to view this question as true or false, depending on their point of view. However, if they are able to adequately support their view, even if it differs from that of the author, then the answer should be evaluated on the display of the student's understanding of the issues.*]

   True. Because the Byzantine Emperor was seen as the ultimate earthly authority, his word was law. When an emperor did not agree with a doctrine or practice (such as the use of icons), he had the power to enforce his decrees within the Orthodox Church. If people did not agree with the emperor and the Orthodox Church, they were fiercely persecuted (whether Nestorians, Monophysites, or iconodules).

3. Match each key person, place, or event on the left side of the page with the short description on the right side of the page.

__g__ Nestorianism	a. Debate over the use of icons
__h__ Mohammed	b. Eastern Roman Empire
__a__ Iconoclast Controversy	c. Christ has only one nature
__j__ Justinian I	d. Capital city of the early Islamic Empire
__d__ Baghdad	e. Golden-mouthed preacher
__i__ Photius the Great	f. Franks defeated Muslim army
__c__ Monophysitism	g. Christ exists as two persons—one human, one divine
__f__ Battle of Tours	h. Founder of Islam
__e__ John Chrysostom	i. Wealthiest, most powerful man since Augustus Caesar
__b__ Byzantine Empire	j. Greatest Byzantine emperor

4. Choose **two** of the following and answer them with a short 1 to 2 paragraph answer. [*The essays written by the student will probably contain at least a few of the following points. If you are unfamiliar with the points actually made by the student, please ask for the sources.*]

   Explain why Byzantine Emperors had so much power, and the effect it had on their reigns.
   - Had legitimacy of rule by continuing line of Roman Empire
   - Believed other kings functioning under them (such as Clovis) did so by their consent
   - Had full power of both the State and the Church, so guided doctrinal issues
   - There were no governing powers except for the emperor to monitor actions
   - No law of succession, so rules usually ended in assassination

   What makes Justinian I one of the greatest of the Byzantine emperors?
   - Ended war with the Persians

Unit 3 Answers

- Ousted Vandals from North Africa and Ostrogoths from Italy
- Raised lots of money and built huge army in face of popular opposition
- Quelled Nika Revolution of 532
- Engaged in massive building program that gained favor with populace
- Built the Hagia Sophia
- Gave official title of Patriarch to head of church in five most important cities
- Wrote *Code of Law*, which simplified existing huge mass of laws
- *Code of Law* still influential in many countries' law books

What was the religious environment that Mohammed was born into and how might it have affected him?
- Polytheists, Christians (of many sects), Jews, Monotheists (Ishmaelites)
- Syrian Christian practice of meditation and prayer for 3 months
- Preached about oneness of God
- Concept was simple and easy to understand—important in light of complex Byzantium Christian doctrines
- After Hegira, no longer focused on truth, but on force/politics

Trace the course of power in the Islamic Empire after Mohammed's death.
- No law of succession, so almost disintegration of Empire
- Successor Caliph Abu Bakr used force to break rebellion and establish order
- First five caliphs elected by a council of elders
- Fifth Caliph Muawiya established hereditary succession with Umayyad dynasty
- After defeat at Battle of Poitiers, Umayyad became unpopular
- Descendant of Mohammed's uncle gained support and overthrew Umayyads
- Abbasid dynasty begun
- Eventually caliphates splinter and begin vying for power

Compare the cities of Constantinople and Baghdad—in what ways are they similar, in what different?
- Both trading cities with strategic locations
- Both very wealthy in an era of relative poverty in Western Europe
- Both hot seats for their respective religions—one Islamic, one Christian
- Both flourishing with arts, sciences, and philosophies
- Constantinople's era of greatness came before Baghdad's
- Baghdad wealthier than Constantinople
- Baghdad built in four years to be capital (to be splendid)

Unit 4 Test
The Holy Roman Empire
& the Vikings

1. Choose **two** of the four Key Concepts below from this Unit with which you are most familiar. For each of these two concepts, list at least two of the most important facts related to that concept. [*Some possible answers are listed below. Accept any reasonable points that were discussed in the reading or audio lessons.*]

Holy Roman Empire

- Began with Pope Leo III crowning Charlemagne emperor
- Married military might of state with Christendom's call to expand the Kingdom
- Counts lineage from Augustus, from Rome to Byzantines to the Franks
- Reestablished a "Christian" empire over Europe in place of barbarian rule

Viking Invasions & Explorations

- First attack, Lindisfarne in 793, and further southward to the holy places of the British Isles
- Attacks marked by plunder, pillage, death, and destruction
- Missions included raiding, trading, and farming
- Attacked divided areas, but not the united Holy Roman Empire under Charlemagne and his son
- After Treaty of Verdun, Western Europe ravaged by Vikings repeatedly
- Dantes eventually defeated by Alfred in England, and their leader, Guthrum, converted to Christianity

Norman Conquest

- Began in 1066 when William the Conqueror invaded England
- William crowned king of England on Christmas day 1066
- Replaced Anglo-Saxon aristocracy with Norman barons
- Introduced strict feudalism based on Norman (French) feudalism

Struggle between Church & State

- In 700s the pope relied on king for protection
- King Pepin gave pope several Lombard cities, thus making him a secular ruler as well
- When Pope Leo III crowned Charlemagne, he claimed power over the state
- People wanted the empire to be the secular arm of the Church, helping her fulfill her mission
- Pope Nicholas I believed that the pope had supremacy over the state.

2. "William the Conqueror was justified in his assault on England." [*Students may choose to view this question as true or false, depending on their point of view. However, if they are able to adequately support their view, even if it differs from that of the author, then the answer should be evaluated on the display of the student's understanding of the issues.*]

- This statement may be argued as true of false. Arguments for William the Conqueror might include his blood ties to the throne of England (his aunt was the mother of the last king of England), and the fact that Harold (who was currently king) had promised to support William's claim to the throne.
- Arguments against William would include his own illegitimate birth, his nationality (French), and the fact that they had already selected a new English king.

3. Match each key person, place, or event on the left side of the page with the short description on the right side of the page.

__f__ Charlemagne		a. Missionaries to the Slavs
__h__ Leif Ericson		b. Church laws regulating warfare
__a__ Cyril & Methodius		c. Norman king of England
__i__ Treaty of Verdun		d. Carried out by Abbot Odo
__e__ Vikings		e. Norse warriors who raided Europe
__g__ Great Schism		f. King of the Franks
__d__ Cluniac Reform		g. 1054
__c__ William the Conqueror		h. Norse explorer
__b__ Peace & Truce of God		i. Divided the Empire into three kingdoms
__j__ Alfred the Great		j. Founder of English nation

4. Choose **two** of the following and answer them with a short 1 to 2 paragraph answer. [*The essays written by the student will probably contain at least a few of the following points. If you are unfamiliar with the points actually made by the student, please ask for the sources.*]

What was so significant about Pope Leo III's action on Christmas Day, 800?
- Unilaterally and unexpectedly decided to crown Charlemagne emperor
- Byzantine emperors had claimed the ownership of the Roman Empire
- But they had not protected Rome in mid-700s, so turned to Frankish Charlemagne's father
- Current ruler of Byzantium was Empress Irene; not recognized because she was a woman and had deposed and blinded her own son
- Western Church looking for emperor to further work of Church
- As pope was growing in power, he needed strong secular power to hold together all of Christendom
- Thus started the Holy Roman Empire
- Raised question if Church has right to make an emperor

What led up to the Treaty of Verdun, and what was its effect?
- Successful passage of power from Charlemagne to son, Louis the Pious
- Louis the Pious divided the Empire in three, with his oldest son acting over his younger brothers
- Younger brothers went to war with Lothair to gain some of his power and territory

- Forced him to sign Treaty of Verdun, which divided kingdom in three (France, Germany, and Lotharingia—or Lorraine)
- Gradually France and Germany began to vie for the territory of Lotharingia
- By 888, further division to France, Germany, Italy, Lorraine, and Burgundy
- Focus of rulers was no longer unity or good rule, but power-grabs at more territory
- Kings gave land to nobles to gain loyalty, resulting in strong nobles and weak kings
- Pope gained authority

What made King Alfred of England different from his western contemporaries?
- United the kingdom
- Held off Vikings
- Invited scholars
- Educated people
- Led people in God's ways

What were the methods and motives of the Viking raiders?
- They first came as raiders, to pillage and plunder
- They attacked using well-built, shallow-bottomed, and swift dragon boats
- They attacked easy targets: undefended monasteries and churches
- They later came as invaders, occupying lands that they conquered
- They also were traders
- They eventually converted to Christianity and ceased their raiding

How did feudalism work?
- The lord or king who owned the land gave some to his vassal in exchange for military service
- He had obligation to protect the people (knights and serfs)
- Vassal knights had to provide military service to the lord
- Serfs had obligation to produce food on master's land, were tied to the land
- Castles were built as the feudal places of protection when under attack

Unit 5 Test
The Crusades & the Mongols

1. Choose **two** of the five Key Concepts below from this Unit with which you are most familiar. For each of these two concepts, list at least two of the most important facts related to that concept. [*Some possible answers are listed below. Accept any reasonable points that were discussed in the reading or audio lessons.*]

The Crusades

- Eight crusades
- People of the time utterly convinced of their righteousness
- Appealed to warriors
- Made sense in medieval Christianity, because paying feudal service to heavenly King
- Few people knew the Bible
- First Crusade is the "People's Crusade"
- 200 years later, last Crusader city (Acre) fell, ending the Latin Kingdoms in the Holy Land
- Deepened divide between Eastern and Western Christianity

Catholic Reformers

- Bernard of Clairvaux, representative of the Cistercian Order, embraced simplicity and poverty
- Francis of Assisi—devoted to living simply, preaching the gospel, and caring for the poor & sick. His new order of mendicant monks (ones who begged for their food and worked in the world rather than living in monasteries) was approved by Pope Innocent III
- Dominic, a Spanish priest, started the Dominicans, a preaching order of monks who were also mendicants. They studied theology above all else, and became influential in the universities of Paris & Rome.

Medieval Dissenters

- Peter Waldo, who started the Waldensians, embraced poverty and the preaching of the gospel. His group was forbidden to preach by the local authorities, and when they continued to do so, they were excommunicated. They went on to rethink the medieval Catholic doctrines, rejecting papal infallibility, purgatory, indulgences, and transubstantiation.
- The Cathars, also known as the Albigensians, were gnostics (similar to those in the early days of the Church). Their beliefs were heretical.

The West in Constantinople

- Great Western Schism where both churches excommunicate the other
- Fourth Crusade in 1204 goes wrong and attacks Constantinople
- Europeans set up Latin Empire of Constantinople

The Mongols

- Genghis Khan united all tribes by 1206 in modern-day Mongolia
- Best army world has seen; modern military generals study tactics

Unit 5 Answers

- Genghis's fear of treachery
- Invincible, terrifying, very violent, much slaughter
- Conquered east to Beijing (and all of China under Kublai Khan); west to Danube
- Tolerated religions
- Both Christian Empire and Islamic Empire "saved by the bell" when khans died on eve of invasion

2. "The Medieval crusades could be conceived of as Christian *jihad*." [**Students may choose to view this question as true or false, depending on their point of view. However, if they are able to adequately support their view, even if it differs from that of the author, then the answer should be evaluated on the display of the student's understanding of the issues.**]

- Many consider this to be true. To those who participated as combatants in the Crusades, a promise was given that their sins would be absolved. The Crusades were a religiously motivated war which appealed to all classes of society. Though it was a religious war called by the leader of the Christian Church, it relied on power of sword, not mental or spiritual weapons. It promoted violent aggression spurred on by ideals, as evidenced by the horrific slaughter of the inhabitants at the end of the siege of Jerusalem in the First Crusade.

3. Match each key person, place, or event on the left side of the page with the short description on the right side of the page.

__g__ Pope Urban II   a. "Holy" wars to rescue the Holy Land from Muslims

__h__ Investiture Controversy   b. Special tribunal to combat and punish heresy

__i__ Thomas Aquinas   c. Venetian explorer who went to China

__f__ Magna Carta   d. Mongolian conqueror

__c__ Marco Polo   e. Muslim leader who took Jerusalem

__j__ Francis of Assisi   f. Charter of English political and civil liberties

__a__ The Crusades   g. Started the First Crusade

__d__ Genghis Khan   h. Power struggle between papacy and Holy Roman Empire

__b__ Inquisition   i. Catholic philosopher/theologian

__e__ Saladin   j. Founder of monastic order

4. Choose **two** of the following and answer them with a short 1 to 2 paragraph answer. [**The essays written by the student will probably contain at least a few of the following points. If you are unfamiliar with the points actually made by the student, please ask for the sources.**]

Describe the change in papal-royal relations.
- Pope Leo III crowns Charlemagne; Pope Gregory VII deposes Emperor Henry IV
- Obedience to God = obedience to pope in high middle ages
- In 1075 Pope Gregory announces series of new laws making papal power ultimate
- Gregory dies in exile and Henry appoints Pope Guibert; Urban II elected by cardinal bishops

Describe the divisions within the Islamic Empire.
- Three different caliphs, one Shi'ite (the Fatimids in Cairo), and the other two Sunni (Abbasid in Baghdad and Umayyad in Cordoba)
- In the Islamic East, Shi'ite warriors called Buyids ruled in place of Abbasid

Unit 5 Answers

- Seljuk Turks convert to Sunni Islam, empire from Iran to Syria/Palestine; eventually capturing Baghdad and the Holy Land
- The Assassins—violent Shi'ite sect—goal to destabilize Sunni government in Eastern empire
- Seljuk Turks divide provinces among many emirs; divided against each other, fell to the crusaders
- United under Saladin

Compare/contrast the first Crusade to the later ones.
- The People's Crusade
- Didn't have maps or scouts, didn't know what to expect
- Successful in achieving goal (at great cost)
- Successive crusades not seen as sure bets; less confidence
- "Perfect timing" for crusaders because of crumbling Seljuk frontiers
- Established Latin kingdoms in Palestine

In what ways did King John (brother of Richard the Lionheart) leave his mark on England?
- He lost the lands in France that had belonged to his family
- He was forced to sign the Magna Carta by his outraged nobles
- He gave England & Ireland to Pope Innocent III, receiving them back as papal fiefs

How did Marco Polo's adventures in China affect Europe?
- Marco, his uncle, and his father all journeyed to Cathay (or China) when Kublai Khan ruled
- Marco Polo traveled extensively in Cathay as a trusted official of the Khan's court
- The Polos returned to Europe after 24 years of travel
- Marco Polo was captured and imprisoned during a war between Genoa & Venice
- During his captivity, he dictated the stories of his travel to a scribe who wrote it all down
- This book became the most widely read book in Europe
- It gave Europeans a desire to have access to the goods of China

Unit 6 Test
Seeds of the Reformation & the Late Middle Ages

1. Choose **two** of the five Key Concepts below from this Unit with which you are most familiar. For each of these two concepts, list at least two of the most important facts related to that concept. [*Some possible answers are listed below. Accept any reasonable points that were discussed in the reading or audio lessons.*]

Hundred Years' War

- David of Scotland (heir to the throne, son of Robert the Bruce) flees to France
- French Nobleman planning revolt, again Philip flees to England
- English longbow instrumental in the English victories at Crécy, Poitier, and Agincourt
- Joan of Arc inspired French troops toward victory, sees French king crowned
- English ultimately lose every territory but Calais

Western Church in Crisis

- Popes fighting with monarchs
- Popes moved to Avignon by Philip the Fair, considered under the influence of France
- Cardinals elect Urban VI (Italian) and Clement VII (French) simultaneously; "Great Western Schism"
- Italian pope had support of northern Italy, England, Scandinavia, and much of Germany while French pope had support of France, Spain, southern Italy, Scotland, and part of Germany—dividing Europe
- Third pope elected and other two officially deposed, but retain power
- Condemn John Wycliffe and John Hus as heretics

The Printing Press

- First press built in 1455
- First book printed on Gutenberg's press is a Bible
- New technology to spread new ideas—especially important into Renaissance
- Books are cheap, become available to everybody, not just rich elites
- Education becomes wide-spread

Exploration & Trade

- Hanseatic League in North Sea and Baltic
- International trading fairs began in Champagne, France
- Italian city states, such as Venice, Genoa, Pisa, and Florence were vitally involved in trade between East and West
- Compass invented in the 1100s; navigational maps of the Mediterranean created
- Prince Henry the Navigator of Portugal opened Age of Exploration
- Cape of Good Hope discovered; opened ocean route to India and Asia
- Inspires Columbus, who headed west towards Asia rather than east

Fall of Constantinople

- Capture of Constantinople during Fourth Crusade weakened the empire greatly
- Byzantine emperors saw the West as their major enemy
- Byzantine army reduced in size, navy disbanded
- Ottoman Turks invited in to support intriguer in Byzantine court
- Ottomans establish foothold in Europe, their territory eventually surrounds Constantinople
- In 1453 Constantinople (last city remaining) falls to the Ottomans
- Greek scholars flee to West—catapulting Europe into the Renaissance

2. **"The relocation of the popes to Avignon opened the door to the Reformation." [Students may choose to view this question as true or false, depending on their point of view. However, if they are able to adequately support their view, even if it differs from that of the author, then the answer should be evaluated on the display of the student's understanding of the issues.]**

- True. As people witnessed the "Babylonian Captivity of the Papacy" and the later "Great Western Schism," it divided Europe into various groups (those who accepted the rule of the pope in France; those who rejected the rule of the pope altogether; and those who accepted the rule of the pope in Italy). This brought about a change of political thinking among many of the rulers of Europe, bringing about a break in the concept of a united "Christendom," where all would follow the decrees of the pope.

3. Match each key person, place, or event on the left side of the page with the short description on the right side of the page.

__h__ John Wycliffe	a. Wars fought between England and France
__c__ Henry the Navigator	b. Ruler of the Ottomans
__j__ Johannes Gutenberg	c. Sent ships down African coast
__i__ Avignon	d. Captured Constantinople
__d__ Ottomans	e. Lifted the siege of Orleans
__b__ Mehmet II	f. 25 million people died in Europe
__e__ Joan of Arc	g. Bohemian reformer and martyr
__a__ Hundred Years' War	h. Translated the Bible into English
__g__ John Hus	i. Seat of seven Popes in the 1300s
__f__ Black Plague	j. Invented the printing press

4. Choose **two** of the following and answer them with a short 1 to 2 paragraph answer. [**The essays written by the student will probably contain at least a few of the following points. If you are unfamiliar with the points actually made by the student, please ask for the sources.**]

What specific examples show how the power of kings decreased from absolute to something less in this age?

- King John in his struggle with pope demonstrates how an English king was no match for the pope
- Magna Carta shows the limiting of a king's power in England
- Emperors trying to rule Italy; divided rule in Germany & Italy

Unit 6 Answers

- Leagues, merchant states outside of the rule of kings
- Powerful Princes in Germany—chose king
- English Parliament holds king in check

Map out the main players in the conflict between Scotland and England, which provides motivations for the Hundred Years War between England and France.

England	Scotland and France
Edward I (King of England)	Scottish lords appointing King
Declares himself king of Scotland	William Wallace leads opposition
Edward III recognizes King	Robert the Bruce becomes King
Claims David's position	David of Scotland unrecognized, flees to Philip VI of France
Welcomes Philip's detractor	
War!	War!

- England's claims to Scottish (twice; Edward I & III) and French thrones
- Scottish revolution; French resistance/defense
- Edward III and Philip VI's decision to accept refugees antagonistic to the other

Summarize John Wycliffe's life and work. What made him stand out in the contemporary Church?

- Preached the Bible as final source on doctrine, against Catholic traditions
- Preached pope is not final authority
- English royalty welcomed him at first because of his popular position that England did not owe pope money as a papal fief
- When he preached against transubtantiation, lost the support of the nobility
- Common people loved him
- Translated Bible into English after losing job at Oxford

How did Joan of Arc aid France during the Hundred Years' War?

- Her visions convinced her that she needed to help Charles get to the north of France (in occupied territory) to be crowned king
- She believed that the French would win the war
- Charles allowed her to take a small army of soldiers to rescue Orléans from the English
- She was able to successfully bring Charles to Rheims to be crowned, which greatly inspired the French people that they would be to be victorious against England

What was the impact of the Black Plague in Europe?

- Between one-third to one-half of the population of Europe died
- It terrified those who lived through it
- Helped to dismantle feudalism
- Had dramatic impact on political, economic, social, and cultural aspects of society

The Renaissance & the Reformation

1. Choose **two** of the five Key Concepts below from this Unit with which you are most familiar. For each of these two concepts, list at least two of the most important facts related to that concept. [*Some possible answers are listed below. Accept any reasonable points that were discussed in the reading or audio lessons.*]

The Renaissance

- High Renaissance in Italy from 1500–1527 (ends when troops sack Rome)
- Renewed interest in Latin language and ancient Roman literature
- Literally "being born again," because ancient writings seem so new from medieval thinking
- When Byzantine scholars come to Europe, people begin learning Greek language
- For first time, western Europeans begin to search for ancient Greek literature and philosophy
- Focus on natural world and humans, resulting in humanism
- Taken from Italy to the rest of Europe
- Typified by artists like Michelangelo, Brunellschi, and da Vinci

The Reformation

- Erasmus translated Bible into Latin from original source documents
- More accurate translation than Vulgate, cleared up some doctrinal issues
- Martin Luther realized that righteousness comes from faith, not works, and that it is possible to walk justly through Jesus's death on the cross
- At same time, Jonathan Tetzel began selling "indulgences"
- October 31, 1517, Luther tacked up the 95 Theses
- Luther's view: whole hierarchy of church unnecessary, people have direct access to God
- Major social and economic implications without hierarchical, feudal system
- Spread quickly throughout Europe

The Age of Exploration

- Some uneducated people believed the world was flat; didn't remember anyone sailing west across Atlantic
- Christopher Columbus convinced Spanish Queen, Isabella, to fund his voyage
- Sailed west to get to India by water route in 1492; discovered South America
- Vasco da Gama, Portuguese navigator, sailed to India south around Africa in 1497
- Major profit from the spices he brought back with him
- Gold from the Americas makes Spain the prominent power in Europe

The New World

- Discovered by Europeans with Christopher Columbus's voyage; called the Indies and Indians incorrectly

- Major source of gold and treasure to Spanish conquistadors
- The desire for gold, spices, and wealth proved a deadly temptation to the Europeans in the New World, which overrode their religious background, resulting in violence, treachery, and cruelty towards the native people
- Vast numbers of native people died as result of contact

The Scientific Revolution

- Copernicus's heliocentric model of the solar system in contrast to geocentric model
- Overthrew the long-held theories of Aristotle and Ptolemy
- Geocentric model had been accepted as true by Catholic Church
- Heliocentric model was seen to be against Catholic dogma, though it was not against Scripture

2. **"The Reformation has had a greater continuing impact on history than the Renaissance."** [*Students may choose to view this question as true or false, depending on their point of view. However, if they are able to adequately support their view, even if it differs from that of the author, then the answer should be evaluated on the display of the student's understanding of the issues.*]

- True. The Renaissance, though it revived humanism and a study of the classics, mainly affected the arts and literature. The Reformation, on the other hand, caused a cataclysmic religious upheaval in the Church, which led to independence of thought on many levels. It also politically impacted European countries deeply, planting the seeds which would become nationalism.

3. Match each key person, place, or event on the left side of the page with the short description on the right side of the page.

__j__ Erasmus	a. Taught heliocentric theory
__h__ Martin Luther	b. Convened to condemn teachings of reformers
__a__ Nicolaus Copernicus	c. Translated English Bible
__b__ Council of Trent	d. Opened route to New World
__i__ Jesuits	e. French reformer
__g__ The Reformation	f. First to circumnavigate the earth
__c__ William Tyndale	g. Initially to reform Catholic Church
__d__ Christopher Columbus	h. Catalyst of the Protestant Reformation
__f__ Ferdinand Magellan	i. Monastic order founded by Ignatius Loyola
__e__ John Calvin	j. Compiled Greek New Testament

4. Choose **two** of the following and answer them with a short 1 to 2 paragraph answer. [*The essays written by the student will probably contain at least a few of the following points. If you are unfamiliar with the points actually made by the student, please ask for the sources.*]

Describe Charles V, and the circumstances at the beginning of his rule.

- Comes to Spanish throne as Charles I, aged 16
- Flemish by birth, but grandchild of Ferdinand & Isabella of Spain
- At same time, Henry VIII becomes king of England and Francis I becomes king of France; Charles related to Henry by marriage, and agrees to marry Francis's daughter (though the wedding's called

off when Charles is elected)
- Emperor Maximilian I dies in 1519, vacating Holy Roman Emperor throne
- German electors select Charles I—becomes Charles V
- Most powerful monarch since Charlemagne:
- Lord of rich and flourishing Netherlands; King of Spain, with part of Italy and American possessions; head of Austrian territories
- Charles and Francis both want England on their side
- Henry VIII decides to renew war with France, so sides with Charles V
- In 1520 Spain and France go to war over who owns land in Italy
- First act of rule is Diet of Worms, where Luther is condemned a heretic

Who is Martin Luther, and what were the radical changes he brought to light?

- German scholar and professor of theology at Wittenberg university
- Read Erasmus's new translation of the Bible into Latin from original Greek
- Realized the "just shall live by faith"—that it's possible to walk righteously through forgiveness from Jesus's death on the cross
- Opposed Johann Tetzel—who sold "indulgences," offering remittance of sin for a price
- Tacked the reasons for his disagreement on the church door—the 95 Theses—October 31, 1517
- Did not intend to be revolutionary, but as church leaders argued with him he responded that people do not need hierarchy of church at all
- Used printing press to spread his ideas among the people
- Condemned a heretic by Charles V, but taken to safety in Germany where he translated Bible into German

What is the significance of Henry VIII?

- King of England
- Married Catherine, daughter of Ferdinand & Isabelle, aunt of Charles V
- Had daughter with Catherine (Mary) but wanted son, so sought annulment to marry Ann Boleyn
- Charles V's soldiers imprisoned Pope Clement VII so he was unwilling to cross Charles by giving Henry the annulment
- Henry married Ann secretly, then had his archbishop declare that marriage to Catherine is void
- England broke completely from Rome
- Henry VIII made Supreme Head of the Church in England
- Had several more wives, and daughter Elizabeth
- Europe was in an uproar!

Compare/contrast Portugal's experience in exploration and trade to Spain's experience.

- Portugal carefully and slowly made their way down the coast of Africa, then went east to the Spice Islands and India
- Spain made one giant leap westward, discovering the New World in the process
- Portugal set up trading outposts in the East, bringing spices back to Europe
- Spain did not get to the spices at all, but found gold and silver

Unit 8 Test
Puritans, Pietists, &
the Divine Right of Kings

1. Choose **two** of the five Key Concepts below from this Unit with which you are most familiar. For each of these two concepts, list at least two of the most important facts related to that concept. [*Some possible answers are listed below. Accept any reasonable points that were discussed in the reading or audio lessons.*]

Europe's Thirty Years' War

- Lasted from 1618 to 1648
- Began as a conflict between Protestants and Catholics, but expanded beyond that
- Bohemian Protestants rebelled following the election of Catholic Ferdinand as King of Bohemia
- Started when the Bohemians threw two Catholic representatives out a tower window (known as the Defenestration of Prague)
- Primarily fought in Germany

British Colonization of New World

- Like Spain and France, England looked beyond its borders of Europe for ways to diversify its income and influence
- In 1607 the first permanent English settlement in America was established at Jamestown, Virginia
- In 1620 Puritan Separatists (knows as the Pilgrims) left England after a decade-long stay in the Dutch Republic to establish a new home in New England
- Many Puritans migrated to America after Charles I became king
- Many colonies were founded in the early- to mid-1600s by Puritans who left England for religious freedom

Galileo & Newton

- Galileo Galilei was a physicist, mathematician, and astronomer
- Galileo improved the telescope and used it in astronomical observations
- Galileo supported the Copernican theory—that the sun is the center of the solar system
- Sir Isaac Newton was a physicist, mathematician, astronomer, and theologian
- Newton was born in the same year that Galileo died
- Newton invented calculus, and described the laws of motion and the universal law of gravitation
- Newton was a Bible-believer and believed in a Creator who had set up the laws of nature

The Puritan Revolution

- Charles I persecuted Puritans in England
- He also alienated many English because of his debt and military problems
- Civil War erupted between the Royalist Cavaliers and the Puritan Roundheads
- Puritans won in 1646
- King Charles I was executed in 1649
- Puritan Oliver Cromwell ruled as Lord Protector of the Commonwealth of England for nine years

Pietism

- Movement in Lutheranism that began in the late 17th century
- Founded by Philipp Jakob Spener
- Pietists viewed Christianity as chiefly consisting in a change of heart and consequent holiness of life
- Pietist Count Von Zinzendorf revived the Moravian church
- This movement inspired John Wesley to begin the Methodist movement

2. "France brought assistance to the Protestants in the Thirty Years' War for religious reasons." [*Students may choose to view this question as true or false, depending on their point of view. However, if they are able to adequately support their view, even if it differs from that of the author, then the answer should be evaluated on the display of the student's understanding of the issues.*]

- False. France's Cardinal Richelieu had one goal: to make France strong. To do that, he decided to send Catholic French troops to fight on the side of the Protestants (his religious enemies) against the Catholic Holy Roman Empire. His strategy worked. At the end of the Thirty Years' War, France received the greatest benefits, and emerged the strongest country in Europe.

3. Match each key person, place, or event on the left side of the page with the short description on the right side of the page.

__h__ John Bunyan	a. The Sun King
__e__ Pilgrims	b. Reformer of Russia
__f__ Edict of Nantes	c. Pioneered telescope in astronomy
__i__ Blaise Pascal	d. Lord Protector of England
__a__ Louis XIV	e. Came to North America seeking religious freedom
__j__ Thirty Years' War	f. Granted rights to Protestants of France
__c__ Galileo Galilei	g. A monarch derives his right to rule from God
__b__ Peter the Great	h. Author of *The Pilgrim's Progress*
__g__ Divine Right of Kings	i. French Christian mathematician
__d__ Oliver Cromwell	j. Religious war in Germany

4. Choose **two** of the following and answer them with a short 1 to 2 paragraph answer. [*The essays written by the student will probably contain at least a few of the following points. If you are unfamiliar with the points actually made by the student, please ask for the sources.*]

Why did the Catholic church condemn Galileo and sentence him to imprisonment, and what can we learn from this episode?

- The Catholic Church, influenced by Greek philosophy, had made the geocentric system of Ptolemy (and Aristotle) a doctrine of the church; to question it was considered heresy.
- Galileo, based on his observations, agreed with Copernicus that the sun, not the earth, was the center of the solar system.
- The Catholic church considered his views heresy and put him on trial, resulting in his imprisonment.
- This affair should make us wary of elevating the teachings and philosophies of men above a sound interpretation of the Word of God. We should hold many of our scientific views and their corresponding Biblical interpretations loosely. For we will never have all the right answers this side of heaven.

Unit 8 Answers

Why did the English Parliament execute Charles I in 1649?

- Charles I was unpopular with the people because he advocated the Divine Right of Kings and levied taxes without the consent of Parliament.
- He married a Catholic princess and allied himself with controversial religious figures, upsetting the Parliament and the Protestant public as well.
- He dismissed Parliament several times when they challenged his arbitrary use of powers.
- Charles I persecuted the Puritans who would not conform to his attempts to impose High Anglican forms of worship, for they considered it too close to Roman Catholicism.
- Finally, civil war broke out. Parliament considered Charles's war against the people of England as treason, and they executed him.

How did Elizabeth I's Act of Uniformity contribute to the rise of the Puritan movement?

- Act of Uniformity was passed by Parliament in 1559.
- This act made it a legal obligation to go to church every Sunday or be fined—a considerable hardship for the poor; it reinforced the Book of Common Prayer to be used in all churches.
- Parts of this act also required that preachers wear certain priestly vestments during church service and dictated how communion was to be celebrated.
- Some Protestants considered that there should be freedom in these matters since they were not mentioned in the Bible.
- This controversy contributed to the rise of the Puritans—those who advocated of "purity" of worship, doctrine, and personal and group morality.
- Puritans felt that the English Reformation had not gone far enough, and that the Church of England retained too many practices associated with Roman Catholicism.

How were the Separatists different from the Puritans?

- The Puritans wanted to reform the Church of England and advocated for purity of worship, doctrine, and morality.
- They recognized the established Church of England, however, and did not believe in separation from the Church, but a reformation from within the Church.
- Separatists were radical Puritans who did not recognize the established Church of England, but rather saw it as corrupt.
- They believed that each church should operate independently, apart form the State (and not subject to its control).
- Separatists had given up on trying to reform the Anglican church; they believed they were chosen of God and wanted to set up an environment where they could worship as they wished.
- The Pilgrims, who came to America in 1620, were Separatists.

What is the basic idea behind the Divine Right of Kings?

- This doctrine holds that a monarch derives his or her right to rule from the will of God, and not from any earthly authority—not from the will of his subjects, the ruling class, or any other part of the realm.
- A monarch is chosen by God, and therefore accountable to Him alone, and need answer only before God for his actions.
- This doctrine also implies that the removal of a monarch or the restriction of his or her powers is contrary to the will of God.

Unit 9 Test
Revivals & Revolutions

1. Choose **two** of the five Key Concepts below from this Unit with which you are most familiar. For each of these two concepts, list at least two of the most important facts related to that concept. [*Some possible answers are listed below. Accept any reasonable points that were discussed in the reading or audio lessons.*]

The Enlightenment

- Also called "age of reason"
- Five basic tenets:
  » Knowledge only comes through our five senses and is interpreted by human reason (no divine revelation)
  » The universe is a machine, following simple, unchangeable laws (no divine intervention)
  » Man is good (no original sin)
  » Nature is good (no curse)
  » If there is a god, he is not involved in the world—Deism
- René Descartes and Voltaire were very influential in elevating human reason above divine revelation
- Influenced much of Europe, and many of the aristocracy

The Great Awakening & Beginning of Abolition

- Move of God in America and Britain
- Focus on personal guilt, public repentance, and personal morality
- George Whitefield, John Wesley, and Jonathan Edwards were the main preachers during this time
- Revival came mainly to the lower classes of society
- Many Christians were involved in the movement to end slavery
- William Wilberforce fought for the abolition of the slave trade in the British Empire

The Seven Years' War

- Fought from 1756 to 1763
- Fought in Europe, American colonies, and in India
- French and Indian War was part of the Seven Years' War
- Prussia, England, British colonies, and Ireland against Austria, Sweden, Russia, and France
- The British and their allies won

Revolutions in France & America

- The American Revolutionary War lasted from 1775 to 1783
- There were many contributing factors to the American Revolution:
  » A growing sense of national unity
  » "Taxation without representation"
  » Fear that the Crown would appoint Anglican bishops over the colonies
  » Oppressive rule by the British monarchy
- The colonists cried out to God to aid them in their struggle
- France allied with the colonies to defeat the British

- The French Revolution lasted from 1789 to 1799
- The causes of the French Revolution included:
  » High taxation
  » Insurmountable national debt
  » High unemployment
- The French turned to Enlightenment philosophy and exalted reason
- Many atrocities accompanied the French Revolution

Cook's Voyages

- Captain James Cook was one of the greatest explorers, navigators, and cartographers in world history
- First voyage (1768–1771): Ship Endeavor searched for southern continent, sailed to Cape Horn, Tahiti, New Zealand, and Australia
- Second voyage (1772–1775): Ship HMS Resolution searched for southern continent, sailed southern latitudes to Tonga, Friendly Islands, Easter Island, Norfolk Island, New Caledonia, and Vanuatu.
- Third voyage (1776–1779): Ship HMS Resolution searched for Northwest Passage, sailed to Tahiti, Sandwich (Hawaiian) Islands, Alaskan coast, Vancouver Island, Aleutian Islands. Cook killed by natives in Hawaii.

2. **"The Great Awakening paved the way for many of the ideas of the American Revolution."** [*Students may choose to view this question as true or false, depending on their point of view. However, if they are able to adequately support their view, even if it differs from that of the author, then the answer should be evaluated on the display of the student's understanding of the issues.*]

Many historians would view this statement as true. Below are some of the ideas that grew from the Great Awakening:

- The Great Awakening was a significant movement, which contributed to a sense of American nationality
- Members of that generation made important choices about their fundamental religious beliefs and loyalties, which may have prepared them to make equally crucial decisions about their political beliefs and loyalties
- The Great Awakening created within the common man a feeling of independence. People assumed new responsibilities in their religious life and became skeptical of dogma and authority
- Many Americans saw the colonies as the "new Israel." They believed that they were God's "chosen people" and this prompted them to perceive the American revolution as a holy war against a sinful, corrupt Britain
- The American political leadership often painted the Revolutionary War in religious terms to attract the support of the religious community

3. Match each key person, place, or event on the left side of the page with the short description on the right side of the page.

__e__ Jonathan Edwards	a. Evangelist of Great Awakening
__i__ The Seven Years' War	b. Invented the steam engine
__a__ George Whitefield	c. Famous explorer
__h__ Charles Wesley	d. Empress of Russia
__f__ John Newton	e. American colonial theologian
__g__ Great Awakening	f. Slave ship captain turned preacher
__c__ Captain Cook	g. Religious revival in England and America
__d__ Catherine the Great	h. Cofounder of Methodism and hymn writer
__j__ George Washington	i. Resulted in England winning French colonial lands
__b__ James Watt	j. First U.S. President

4. Choose **two** of the following and answer them with a short 1 to 2 paragraph answer. [*The essays written by the student will probably contain at least a few of the following points. If you are unfamiliar with the points actually made by the student, please ask for the sources.*]

What are the main elements of "Enlightenment" thinking?
- Knowledge only comes through our five senses and is interpreted by human reason (no divine revelation)
- The universe is a machine, following simple, unchangeable laws (no divine intervention)
- Man is good (no original sin)
- Nature is good (no curse)
- If there is a god, he is not involved in the world—Deism

What were the main differences between the American Revolution and the French Revolution?
- American revolutionaries cried out to God for help; French looked to the "goddess" of human reason and strength
- American revolution grew out of ideas from the Great Awakening; French Revolution grew out of ideas of the Enlightenment
- Americans drew other countries to their aid; the French were isolated and other European countries viewed the revolution with horror
- Many atrocities accompanied the French Revolution; not so with the American Revolution

Relate some of the accomplishments of John Wesley.
- Ministered for over 50 years
- Preached over 42,000 sermons
- Traveled over 250,000 miles throughout England, Scotland, and Ireland
- Published over 200 books
- Encouraged William Wilberforce in his fight to stop the slave trade
- Called "Father of the Great Awakening in England;" cofounder of Methodism

Why did Prussia go to war against Austria?
- Frederick II was a student of the Enlightenment
- Frederick was an absolute ruler and there was no one to stop him
- The area of Austria he attacked (Silesia) was a rich, prosperous land
- His opponent, Empress Maria Theresa, did not present the same threat to Frederick that her father Charles VI had
- Maria Theresa gathered allies against Prussia in order to win back Silesia, so Frederick attacked first
- The War of Austrian Succession led to the Seven Years' War